SCIENCE ESSENTIALS CHEMISTRY

Fuels and the Environment

DENISE WALKER

Evans

EVANS
LONDON

© Evans Brothers Ltd 2007

Published by:
Evans Brothers
2a Portman Mansions
Chiltern Street
London W1U 6NR

Series editor:
Harriet Brown

Editor:
Katie Harker

Design:
Robert Walster

Illustrations:
Peter Bull Art Studio
Ian Thompson

Printed in China by
WKT Company Limited

British Library Cataloguing in
Publication Data

Walker, Denise
  Fuels and the environment. -
  (Science essentials. Chemistry)
  1. Air - Pollution - Juvenile literature
  2. Fossil fuels - Environmental
  aspects - Juvenile literature 3.
  Greenhouse gases - Juvenile literature
  I. Title
  577.2'76

ISBN-10: 0-237-52999-8
ISBN-13: 978-0-237-52999-4

Contents

Introduction

Fuels have become an important part of our daily lives. Without fuels we would be unable to heat our homes or cook food. We depend on fuels to

run our cars, buses, trains and aeroplanes. Some fuels are used to produce electricity, to power lights and other appliances in our homes. Refined fuels are also used to make many everyday products.

This book takes you on a journey to discover more about the wonderful world of fuels. Find out about different types of fuel, discover how we access and refine them for our own needs and learn about the impact that fuels have on the environment. You can also find out about famous scientists, like Charles Goodyear and Leo Baekeland. Learn how they used their skills to make rubber and plastic from fuels – materials that have come to revolutionise our lives.

This book also contains feature boxes that will help you to unravel more about the mysteries of fuels and the environment. Test yourself on what you have learnt so far; investigate some of the concepts discussed; find out more key facts; and discover some of the scientific findings of the past and how these might be utilised in the future.

Fuels are a vital part of modern life but it is important that we use them carefully to protect our natural world. Now you can understand why the race is on to find alternative fuels for the future – to replace the fuels that we have used and to ensure that we minimise the impact that fuels have on the environment.

Did you know?

▶ Watch out for these boxes – they contain surprising and fascinating facts about fuels and our environment.

Test yourself

▶ Use these boxes to see how much you've learnt. Try to answer the questions without looking at the book, but take a look if you are really stuck.

Investigate

▶ These boxes contain experiments that you can carry out at home. The equipment you will need is usually cheap and easy to find around the home.

Time travel

▶ These boxes describe scientific discoveries from the past and fascinating developments that pave the way for the advance of science in the future.

Answers

At the end of this book on pages 46 and 47, you will find the answers to the questions from the 'Test yourself' and 'Investigate' boxes.

Glossary

Words highlighted in **bold** are described in detail in the glossary on pages 46 and 47.

What are fuels?

1

A fuel is any substance that is used to release heat and/or light energy. We use fuels to heat our homes, to cook our food and to generate electricity. Fuels also help to run the vehicles that we use to move people and goods from place to place, around the world, and up into space.

▶ We use fuels to make electricity and to power our vehicles.

Many fuels release heat and light energy through **combustion reactions** – they burn in oxygen to release energy, as well as a number of chemical products.

▲ Wood is a traditional fuel used for cooking and heating.

Many of the fuels that we use in everyday life are called **fossil fuels**. Fossil fuels are made from the remains of prehistoric plants and animals that have become buried beneath the Earth's surface over millions of years. Fossil fuels, such as **crude oil**, coal and natural gas, have been used for thousands of years. The Ancient Chinese and Egyptians, for example, are known to have burned oil to light their lamps around 1500 BCE.

DIFFERENT TYPES OF FUEL

Throughout history, many different substances have been used as fuels (depending on the availability of materials in a particular area). Here are just some of the fuels that we use:

▶ **Coal** – In 2005, coal provided about 26 per cent of the energy needed worldwide. Most of our coal reserves are used to generate electricity. China and the USA are rich in coal supplies, but scientists estimate that at current rates there are only 252 years of coal supplies left worldwide.

▶ **Crude oil** – In 2005, oil provided about 35 per cent of the world's energy needs. Almost 90 per cent of vehicles are powered by petrol or diesel – **refined** products of crude oil. Oil can also be used to generate electricity and is the source of many industrial chemicals. However, there are only an estimated 32 years of oil supplies left.

▶ **Natural gas** – In 2005, natural gas provided about 25 per cent of the world's energy needs. Gas is used for heating homes as well as for some industrial processes. Gas can be transported through pipelines and costs about the same as petrol. Gas has been a plentiful fuel, but scientists think there are only about 72 years of supplies left.

▶ **Propane** – Propane is found in crude oil and in natural gas. It can be used for heating, cooking, lighting and industrial purposes. As a liquefied gas, propane can also be used to fuel vehicles.

▶ **Ethanol** – Ethanol is made by **fermenting** sugar (which can be made from corn or sugar cane). For many years, ethanol has been used in the USA and Brazil as a fuel to power vehicles (see page 37) by combining it with petrol.

▶ **Methanol** – Methanol is a very similar **compound** to ethanol and can be made from the fermentation of sugars, as well as from wood. Methanol is sometimes mixed with petrol and used as a fuel for high performance racing cars because it burns efficiently.

▶ **Biomass** – This is a term used to describe energy from the Sun that becomes incorporated into animals and plants via the **food chain**. Sources of biomass include farming waste and animal faeces. Biomass can be used to generate electricity (see page 45).

FOSSIL FUELS

Three of the most important fuels that we use today are coal, crude oil and natural gas. Crude oil and natural gas form over millions of years from the remains of dead animals and coal comes from the remains of dead plants. Fossil fuels are called **non-renewable** fuels because they are used much faster than they can be replaced. This means that they are in danger of running out.

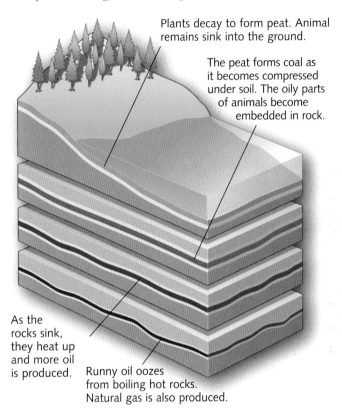

Plants decay to form peat. Animal remains sink into the ground.

The peat forms coal as it becomes compressed under soil. The oily parts of animals become embedded in rock.

As the rocks sink, they heat up and more oil is produced.

Runny oil oozes from boiling hot rocks. Natural gas is also produced.

▲ Fossil fuels form over millions of years from the remains of dead plants and animals.

DID YOU KNOW?

▶ Scientists have calculated how much energy we use to fuel our cars in comparison to the remains of dead animals. The average car tank can hold 55 litres of fuel. Scientists estimate that this is equivalent to the distilled remains of 225 elephants! These figures may seem high, but we must remember that fuel is only made from a small percentage of an animal's remains (on average 1 part in 10,000). These remains begin to form a fuel over about 500 million years.

▶ Legend has it that in ancient times, people saw mysterious fires coming from the ground. These fires were thought to be signs from the gods or the symbol of an invisible god (as believed by the Zoroastrian religion, for example). However, today scientists believe that the fires were probably fuelled by natural gas. During a thunderstorm, for example, it would be possible for lightning to set fire to natural gas that had escaped from beneath the Earth's crust.

HYDROCARBONS

Fossil fuels are also called **hydrocarbons**. This is because, in their pure form, they contain only the elements carbon and hydrogen – elements that are released from the remains of dead organisms.

When hydrocarbons burn to release energy (in the form of heat and light) they also release chemical products. The hydrogen part of the fuel burns in oxygen to form water (which is given off as steam because the reaction is at a high temperature). The carbon part of the fuel burns in oxygen to release carbon dioxide. If the fuel is burning in a small amount of oxygen, carbon monoxide may be released instead.

DEMONSTRATING COMPLETE COMBUSTION

If a fuel burns in a plentiful supply of oxygen, we say that complete combustion occurs. This is when all of the hydrocarbon parts of a fuel burn to produce their chemical products. The diagram below shows that the products of complete combustion are carbon dioxide and water.

When the candle is lit, it is placed quite close to the funnel so it will burn with a strong orange flame and produce little smoke – this shows that almost complete combustion is occurring. The candle wax is an example of a hydrocarbon fuel and is useful for this experiment because we can control the amount of fuel that is used.

When the water pump is switched on, air from the burning candle is drawn through the equipment. The air contains the products of combustion. First, the air passes through an empty (but very cold) U-tube. This causes some of the components to **condense**. The air then passes through some limewater and we see lots of bubbles. Very quickly, the limewater turns milky, indicating the presence of carbon dioxide.

At the end of the experiment, the U-tube contains a colourless liquid. If you add this liquid to anhydrous cobalt chloride, the solution turns pink, indicating the presence of water.

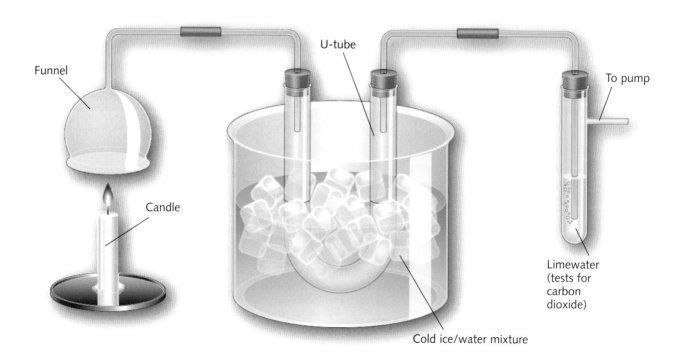

Funnel

Candle

U-tube

To pump

Limewater (tests for carbon dioxide)

Cold ice/water mixture

DEMONSTRATING INCOMPLETE COMBUSTION

If we hold the candle closer to the funnel, a much smokier flame occurs because the funnel limits the supply of oxygen. This smoke is un-burnt carbon. The limewater also remains unchanged and colourless for much longer, showing that very little carbon dioxide has been given off. Instead, a more deadly gas, called carbon monoxide, has been produced (CO). Water, however, is still collected.

Complete and incomplete combustion can also be observed in a laboratory with a Bunsen burner. If we open the air hole of a burner there is a good supply of oxygen and complete combustion occurs (the flame is bright blue and no soot appears on heated apparatus). If the air hole is only partially opened, however, the supply of oxygen is lower. The products in this instance are water and carbon (soot), some carbon monoxide and much less carbon dioxide.

▲ ▶ An orange flame on a Bunsen burner shows that incomplete combustion is occurring, whereas a bright blue flame indicates complete combustion due to a more plentiful supply of oxygen.

CARBON MONOXIDE

Incomplete combustion can occur in many of the petrol-fuelled vehicles on our roads. This can be seen when clouds of black smoke are expelled from exhaust pipes. Some vehicles carry out a combination of both incomplete and complete combustion – when both carbon dioxide and carbon monoxide are released from the exhaust.

Carbon monoxide is a deadly gas that is difficult to detect because it is colourless and odourless. Carbon monoxide interferes with the transportation of oxygen around the body. When we breathe in carbon monoxide, the gas binds to the red blood cells in our body – blood cells that usually carry oxygen gas. If enough red blood cells are occupied by carbon monoxide, it can be fatal.

Fortunately, when petrol fumes reach the atmosphere, the carbon monoxide is dispersed in the air and becomes less dangerous. Carbon monoxide can be a problem in our homes, however, if gas appliances are faulty and there is poor ventilation. Gas cookers and central heating boilers need to be checked regularly to ensure complete combustion is taking place.

2

Accessing fossil fuels

Fossil fuels are generally found deep beneath the Earth's surface. For this reason, their extraction is not always easy. Over the years, various techniques have been developed in our quest to obtain these precious fuels.

COAL

Coal is formed from the remains of prehistoric trees, ferns and other plants. Over millions of years, the remains were crushed into the earth and became compressed by layers of rocks and sediment above them. Slowly, the remains decayed and coal was left behind.

Coal is formed in a variety of stages. The initial form of coal is called peat. This soft brown material is similar to coal but has had less time to compact and decompose. Peat contains about 70 per cent water. It is found near to the Earth's surface and is sometimes used locally as a fuel for heating homes and for cooking.

▲ Peat is found near to the Earth's surface and can be harvested using farming machinery.

If peat is left in the ground for longer it becomes lignite – another form of coal. Lignite is much harder than peat. It contains approximately 55 per cent carbon and 35 per cent water. Eventually, anthracite is formed. This very hard material is almost 100 per cent carbon – the best grade of coal.

The USA has the world's largest known coal reserves – about 275 billion tonnes. However, since scientists believe that world coal reserves will decline dramatically over the next 250 years, this resource will be more heavily drawn upon. Around one billion and 100 million tonnes of coal are currently mined in the USA and the UK respectively, each year.

COAL EXTRACTION

In the USA and the UK, most coal deposits are found at a depth of several hundred metres. This coal is extracted by underground mining when boreholes and mines are burrowed into the ground. The mines are large enough to take people and vehicles, and are supported by a great deal of steel work for safety. Coal is removed from the surrounding rock and transported to the surface.

▼ This technician is measuring the noise levels produced by machinery in a coal mine. Mine workers have to wear ear defenders to protect themselves against hearing loss.

In other parts of the world where coal is much closer to the surface, surface mining can be used instead. Surface mining involves the use of heavy machinery to move surface earth and to excavate the coal. This type of mining leaves piles of earth behind. We call these 'spoil banks'.

In areas where coal is buried very deep beneath the Earth's surface, a new type of coal mining technique, called mountaintop removal, is used. In some regions of the world – such as West Virginia, USA – this is the only type of coal left. In this method, the tops of hills are excavated down to 300 metres and the remaining land is levelled using explosives. This type of mining is very destructive to the landscape.

▲ Heavy machinery is used to excavate coal at this surface coal mine in central Asia.

USES FOR COAL

Today, around 80 per cent of coal is used in power stations, mostly to generate electricity. Coal is also used to power industrial processes, such as steel-making furnaces. Some domestic customers use coal fires to heat their homes. Many countries also export their coal reserves for these uses.

Coal is often refined to make it into a cleaner fuel. When coal is heated in the absence of air, impurities (such as coal tar and coal gas) are removed. Refined coal is called 'coke' and burns without producing smoke.

TIME TRAVEL: DISCOVERIES OF THE PAST

▶ Scientists have developed a technique that produces synthetic oil from coal or natural gas. In the Fischer-Tropsch process, a mixture of carbon monoxide and hydrogen (from coal or gas) are reacted together to produce a synthetic fuel oil. The technique is often used in countries, such as South Africa, that are rich in coal deposits.

The process was first invented in Germany during the 1920s. Although Germany had very little fuel, it had large coal deposits. Today, a handful of companies are using the technology. SASOL, for example, produces most of South Africa's diesel by using coal and natural gas resources. This technology is likely to become increasingly important as oil deposits decline.

Before oil began to be used commercially in the 1800s, animal fats (such as whale fat) were burnt in torches and lamps to produce heat and light. However, animal fats were expensive (an equivalent of US$760 per litre at today's prices), so only the wealthy could afford them. Soon, people began to search for cheaper alternatives and in 1857, Michael Dietz invented the kerosene lamp. Kerosene was initially refined from oil that had seeped from the ground or could be extracted from rocks. It was cheaper than whale fat, burnt cleanly, smelt better and did not decompose. Kerosene lamps were used until 1879 when the electric light bulb was invented.

FINDING OIL

China was probably the first country to use oil. In around 300 CE, for example, China was known to have extracted oil by drilling a hole (or well) to a depth of over 200 metres, using a drill attached to a bamboo pole. The Chinese used the heat from burning oil to evaporate water from brine to produce salt. However, the more modern approach to oil extraction is considered to have begun in the 1800s.

In 1855, the first oil wells were opened in Ontario, Canada and by 1910, a number of large Canadian oil reserves were being explored. At this time, oil wells were also opened in the East Indies, Persia (now Iran), Peru and Venezuela. The demand for oil was increasing around the world – largely due to the invention of motor vehicles.

Oil has now been extracted from the ground for over 100 years and supplies are becoming increasingly difficult to find. Locating a source of oil is a precise science. Although oil naturally rises to the surface in some parts of the world – such as in remote parts of Alaska – on the whole, more precise exploratory techniques need to be employed.

When an exploration company looks for a new oil well, it will search for obvious surface features, such as oil or gas seeps – natural springs where oil or gas leak out of the ground. There are also features called pockmarks that form when gas escapes in these regions.

▲ This heavy oil is seeping through the sand at Vertal in Utah, USA. An estimated 28 billion barrels of oil are thought to be available from sand deposits in Utah.

If these features are not apparent, a company will rely instead on more sophisticated methods. At first, aircraft and satellite photographs may indicate geographical features that suggest the presence of oil or gas. If this is the case, the first test will be a gravity and magnetic survey. In a gravity survey, a gravimeter is used to detect changes in the Earth's gravitational field. These changes may be due to small vibrations caused by the activity of fuels beneath. During a magnetic search, a magnetometer is used to measure the strength of the Earth's magnetic field. These changes can be caused by the presence of different rocks beneath the Earth's surface, which might indicate the presence of oil.

▲ A computer representation of oil deposits (shown in red) in rocks beneath the Earth's surface.

If the results of these searches look promising, a seismic survey will then be carried out. During this survey, sound waves are projected into the Earth's crust and scientists record the time taken for them to be reflected back from rocks underground. This creates a picture of the type and density of rock in any given place.

The last stage in finding oil is an experimental drill. If the seismic survey is encouraging, an experimental hole is drilled. If oil is found, mass **spectroscopy** can also be used to test the molecules in an oil sample. This can help to determine the age of the sample and to predict the logistics of bringing oil to the surface. The whole process can be very expensive and there is no guarantee that success will be achieved. Once oil has been found, the cost of setting up a well to extract the oil reserves can range from US$10 million to US$100 million, depending on location.

OIL EXTRACTION

Once an oil deposit has been discovered, it will be subjected to four stages:

▶ **Drilling** – An oil rig drills a hole between 10 and 75 centimetres wide. A metal pipe, slightly smaller than the hole, is then inserted to ensure that the hole will not collapse. The hole is then drilled deeper. This is repeated until a suitable depth has been achieved. Sometimes, oil rigs are constructed at sea. These 'offshore' oil rigs can be the size of villages and workers live on the rigs for months at a time.

▶ **Completion** – During this stage, holes are drilled in the side of the metal piping to allow oil from surrounding rocks to flow into the main drilled hole. Acids and fluids are also injected into the drill hole to encourage the oil to flow out of the surrounding rocks.

▶ **Production** – In this stage, oil and gas are extracted. The high pressure in the narrow drill hole causes oil to rise to the surface. Oil can also be extracted from the ground using a mechanical pump.

▶ **Abandonment** – Once all the oil has been extracted, the well is abandoned – the hole is simply filled with cement.

▲ A drilling rig can be used to drill hundreds of metres into the ground.

▼ Nodding donkeys are a type of pump used to extract oil from beneath the Earth's surface.

THE JOURNEY OF FOSSIL FUELS

Once crude oil, natural gas and coal have been mined, they need to be transported to consumers who will use them. Unfortunately, many of these stages cause environmental damage. Mining itself can be destructive to the landscape, but transportation can make the problem even worse. Some of the problems associated with mining are outlined below. This is not an exhaustive list, but nevertheless gives a good idea of the impact of mining.

▶ **Dust pollution** – One of the consequences of an explosion is the fallout dust that follows. People who are sensitive to dust may become more vulnerable to lung diseases, such as asthma.

▶ **Air pollution** – Lorries and other vehicles on site can increase the amount of dust that circulates and exhaust fumes can pollute the air.

▶ **Destruction of land and habitat** – When a mine is abandoned, the area may never return to its original form. This is especially true for mountaintop removal. If a landscape has been changed, local habitats will also have suffered, sometimes permanently. Mining can also leave behind waste materials, such as scrap metal, acids, solvents and diesel fuel.

▶ **Noise pollution** – Explosives that are used to free a fossil fuel (such as coal) from rock can be very loud. This can disturb people living nearby and can be terrifying for animals in the area.

▲ Mining blasts can produce both air and noise pollution, causing difficulties for those living nearby.

TIME TRAVEL: INTO THE FUTURE

▶ Scientists have been looking at new ways to drill for oil and gas that are kinder to the environment. In the future, powerful laser beams of light may be used to drill into the ground. Scientists are also looking at ways to send robots to the bottom of the ocean to drill for oil, instead of building large offshore oil rigs.

▶ The Arctic could be a useful new source of natural gas. Scientists have found samples of natural gas in wet snow and ice in the Arctic region and it is believed that more gas lies undiscovered in the area. However, there are concerns that extracting the gas could cause serious damage to this natural habitat.

▲ Oil tankers are a cheap way to transport oil, but an oil spill could be environmentally and economically costly.

TRANSPORTATION

Pipelines were first used to move oil and gas around the world in the late 1800s. Once a pipeline has been set up, it is a very economical way of transporting large amounts of oil and gas. It is cheaper than using road or rail because large quantities of fuel can be continuously transported.

Pipelines are mostly used on land. They can be built under the sea, but construction is difficult and tanker ships may be more economical. Oil is transported using either steel or plastic pipes that vary from 0.3 to 1.2 metres in diameter.

▼ Pumps are used to move oil through pipelines at average speeds of four metres per second.

The pipelines are usually built above the surface, but when they come close to urban or environmentally-sensitive areas, they are buried about one metre underground. Gas pipes follow the same principle, but are slightly thinner.

Pipelines transport valuable fuels around the world but they have one major disadvantage – fuels are explosive. When explosive material is transported, there is always the risk of an accident. In 1989, for example, sparks from two passing trains ignited a gas leak from a pipeline in Russia, killing 645 people. Pipelines have to be checked regularly to prevent accidents of this kind. Pipelines are also vulnerable to terrorist attack.

DID YOU KNOW?

▶ A 1,200 kilometre pipeline runs along the seabed from Norway to the UK. Gas travels along this pipeline at about 24 kilometres an hour!
▶ Ships that carry oil and gas are specially made so that they are less likely to leak if a collision occurs. The tankers have a 'double hull' as added protection. Empty spaces in the hull are also filled with a type of gas that does not catch fire.

Refining fossil fuels

Chemists have discovered a variety of ways in which the products of crude oil, natural gas and coal can be used. Once these fossil fuels are transported from their source, they need to be processed further to make them desirable to consumers.

HOW DO WE USE FOSSIL FUELS?

▶ **Transport** – Internal combustion engines are used in a variety of modern vehicles, from cars to trains. These engines use the energy from ignited petrol or diesel to push pistons. In aeroplanes, aviation fuel is used to power jet engines. These fuels are all types of refined crude oil.

▲ Aeroplane engines use a type of refined crude oil.

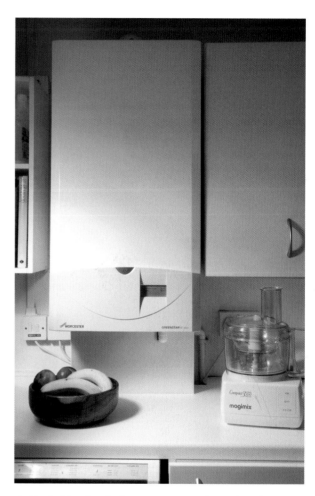

▲ Central heating boilers are common in western homes.

▶ **Heating** – Some people burn coal to heat their homes. However, many homes now use central heating, powered by oil or gas. Houses are built with a system of pipes linked to radiators, containing water. When the central heating is switched on, the oil or gas burns and releases energy which heats the water. As the water flows through the system, this heat is given off in each room through the radiators.

▶ **Electricity** – Most power stations use combustible fuels, such as coal and oil, to heat water to turn it into steam. The steam drives turbines (giant rotating shafts) and these in turn work generators that convert the movement into an electrical current. A network of power lines then transports the electricity to our homes to be used whenever it is needed.

▶ **New materials** – Much of our everyday lives are filled with plastic. If you just consider the room that you are currently sitting in, you may be able to see at least ten different types of plastic. Plastic is a relatively new material, produced from crude oil (see page 24). Oil can also be used to make a wide range of products such as paints, fertilisers, medicines, lubricants, synthetic rubber tyres for vehicles, and candles.

▶ **Cooking** – Whilst some cookers are powered by electricity, others are fuelled by natural gas. The gas is mainly composed of **methane** and is similar to the gas used in laboratory Bunsen burners. Natural gas is odourless and for safety reasons a natural chemical 'odorant' is added which smells a bit like rotten eggs. This means that dangerous gas leaks can be detected by smell.

▲ Many homes now have a gas supply for cooking and heating purposes.

Other fuels used for cooking include butane and propane. These gases have been cooled to liquefy them and can be bought in canisters for camping stoves and caravans. Both these fuels are derived from crude oil.

SMOKELESS FUELS

During the 1800s, a lot of coal was burnt in cities for heating, but the air became thick with black dust and smoke. Today, some towns and cities only allow 'smokeless' fuel to be burnt as a domestic fuel, to prevent air pollution problems of this kind. Coke is an example of a smokeless fuel. Coke is difficult to light, but it burns with a 'clean' blue flame, and produces only a small amount of soot. To make smokeless fuels, coal is heated in an enclosed environment to drive off pollutant tars (see page 11). Whilst it is still hot, the coke is shaped into convenient briquettes.

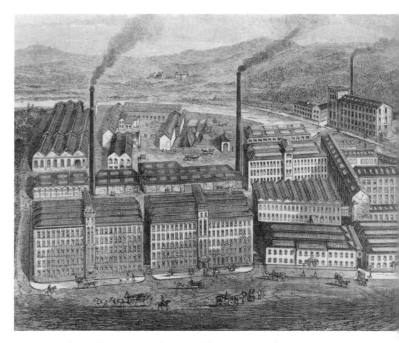

▲ During the Industrial Revolution of the 1700s and 1800s, factories produced polluting smoke as productivity increased.

INVESTIGATE

▶ The fuels we choose often depend on the amount of energy they produce. Ask your teacher to help you to compare the amount of energy in ethanol and paraffin.

Burn equal quantities of each fuel to heat two beakers of water. Test the temperature of the water in each beaker before and after the experiment. Which fuel heats the water the most?

REFINING CRUDE OIL

Crude oil is a mixture of hydrocarbons. These compounds come from the dead organisms from which crude oil is made and contain only hydrogen and carbon atoms. Some hydrocarbons are described as 'short-chain' because they contain very few carbon and hydrogen atoms (or the ones they have are grouped together). Others are described as 'long-chain' because they contain many more atoms in long chains.

In its pure form, crude oil is not very useful. However, the compounds from which crude oil is made can be very valuable. Drilling companies will either sell the crude oil to another company for refining, or carry out the refining process themselves. The latter is more favourable because there is more profit to be made from selling refined crude oil products.

FRACTIONAL DISTILLATION OF CRUDE OIL

When crude oil is refined, it is heated and passed through fractional distillation equipment that separates the components according to their boiling points. The oil undergoes each of the following stages:

▶ Crude oil is first heated as it passes into the column. The hydrocarbons that are shortest will evaporate first because they have the lowest boiling points. They will travel to the top of the column before condensing and being collected. Typically this fraction has no more than four carbon atoms and is called petroleum gas.

▶ The hydrocarbons with the next lowest boiling point will then evaporate and travel near to the top of the column. This fraction has between 4 and 8 carbons atoms and is called petrol. This is the fuel that we use in our cars.

FRACTIONAL DISTILLATION

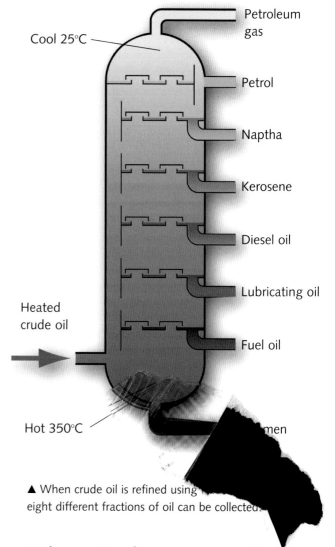

▲ When crude oil is refined using eight different fractions of oil can be collected.

▶ The remaining fractions evaporate off as their boiling points are reached and they are separated in turn.

The fractions that follow petrol are:
(1) Naptha (8-10 carbon atoms).
(2) Kerosene (10-16 carbon atoms).
(3) Diesel oil (16-20 carbon atoms).
(4) Lubricating oil (20-30 carbon atoms).
(5) Fuel oil (30-40 carbon atoms).
(6) Bitumen (more than 50 carbon atoms).

Each of these fractions has its own individual uses, summarised by the table opposite.

Fraction	Use
Petroleum gas	Can be used to make methane
Petrol	Fuel for cars
Naptha	Used to make chemicals/medicines
Kerosene	Fuel for aircraft
Diesel oil	Central heating and vehicle fuel
Lubricating oil	Oil for machinery
Fuel oil	Fuel for power stations
Bitumen	Surfacing for roads

TEST YOURSELF

(1) Mark distils some crude oil in the laboratory but then gets confused about the order of the fractions that he has extracted. How can Mark decide which fraction is which?

(2) Write down all the fractions of crude oil on different pieces of paper. Shuffle the papers and try to put the fractions back into the correct order, from the lightest to the heaviest fraction.

LABORATORY DISTILLATION OF OIL

You can perform fractional distillation in a laboratory, on a much smaller scale. Sometimes, scientists soak a sample of glass wool with crude oil and then heat it using a Bunsen burner. When the first oil fraction evaporates it condenses into a small test tube that is then removed and replaced with another for the next fraction. Another way to carry out fractional distillation is to use a glass column filled with glass beads. As the oil evaporates it passes through the column and the beads provide a large and cool surface area on which the oil fraction condenses to form a liquid. The heat then causes the liquid to evaporate again and recondense further up the column, where it can be collected.

As each fraction is collected, they become increasingly dark in colour and thicker to pour. These properties are related to the number of carbon atoms that each fraction contains – the larger the number of carbon atoms, the darker and thicker the fraction.

▲ These glass beads provide a large, cool surface area on which the fractions of evaporated oil can condense. Oil can be separated in a laboratory on a small scale.

USING THE FRACTIONS

▶ **Petroleum gas/petrol** – Petrol is commonly used today as a fuel for the majority of cars on our roads. Before the invention of cars in the mid-1800s, petrol was sold in small vials and used as a treatment against lice.

Additives are put into petrol to make it even more useful. The table below shows the reasons why some additives are added:

Additive	Reason
Lead	Used to be added to petrol so it did not ignite too soon in the engine. Not used any more because of the dangers of lead poisoning.
MMT (methyl cyclopentadienyl manganese tricarbonyl)	Helps cars that are designed to run on leaded fuel, to now run on unleaded fuel that is kinder to the environment.
Oxygenates	Reduces the amount of carbon monoxide produced in the exhaust fumes.

▶ **Kerosene** – Kerosene was traditionally used in kerosene lamps (right) before the invention of electricity (see page 12). Kerosene is also used as an aviation fuel, and can sometimes be used in portable camping stoves. As kerosene has more carbon atoms in its molecules than petrol, the molecules are bigger. The oil is thicker because the larger molecules tangle up with each other easily and are difficult to separate. The large molecules have higher boiling and melting points because more energy is needed to separate the individual molecules.

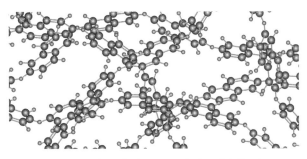

▲ Heavy molecules of oil are tangled and difficult to separate. This makes the liquid very thick.

▶ **Diesel oil** – Diesel can be pumped and is a useful fuel for running vehicles. Because diesel is thicker than kerosene, it is also a useful lubricant for the engine. Larger vehicles usually run on diesel because it burns efficiently over long distances. One of the first diesel vehicles was driven for nearly 1,200 kilometres in the 1930s without a pit stop! Diesel vehicles have a reputation for being 'sluggish' but technology has now developed to prevent this – to such an extent that in the last two decades, some racing cars have begun to use diesel fuel. In 2006, for example, a British diesel-powered vehicle broke records by reaching speeds of around 560 kilometres per hour.

▶ **Fuel oil** – This is a very thick product and can only just be classed as a liquid. Fuel oil is used to power ships that travel great distances before they can be re-fuelled. Fuel oil burns quite slowly and releases a lot of energy. However, it does not burn very cleanly and would therefore be unsuitable for use in our towns and cities.

▶ **Lubricating oil** – Lubricating oil is thicker than diesel. Lubricating oil also appears to be more 'oily' if you examine samples of both.

▲ Car engines need regular oiling to keep the parts moving smoothly and to stop them wearing away.

Lubricating oil is used to oil the surfaces of moving parts. Lubricated surfaces move more freely together, preventing friction from wearing them away. Lubricating oils can also prevent the formation of rust in machinery.

▶ **Bitumen** – This is the last fraction of crude oil and therefore has the highest boiling point. The molecules in bitumen are long and because they become tangled, bitumen is classed as a solid. Bitumen is used in the paving of roads because it is strong enough to withstand heavy traffic.

DID YOU KNOW?

▶ A fraction of crude oil is known to be an effective remedy against intestinal worms. Swallowing up to two tablespoons of kerosene is said to destroy the parasites that can be contracted from infected food – but don't try this out for yourself!

However, on very hot days, the road surfaces may soften slightly. Bitumen is very waterproof and can be used in the construction of roofs; this is especially important on flat roofs, to prevent leaks in wet weather.

▶ **Naptha** – Naptha is mainly used in the manufacture of chemicals and medicines. However, naptha is sometimes used as an ingredient in shoe polish and as a fuel for portable stoves and lanterns.

PARAFFIN WAXES

Paraffin waxes can also be made from crude oil. The molecules in paraffin waxes have lots of carbon atoms, causing them to be long and very tangled. They are actually termed as 'solids' because so much energy is required to untangle the mass of molecules. Paraffin waxes are used to make candles, moisturisers and some food additives. Paraffin wax is also added to some sweets to make them look shiny!

▲ Many candles are made from paraffin wax. This fuel is useful because it burns very slowly.

CRACKING

You may notice that some of the fractions of oil are in high demand, whereas others are in less demand. Lubricating oil, for example, is less useful than petrol. Fortunately, it is possible for companies to refine oil even further to meet the demands of their customers. For example, petrol can be made by separating some of the heavier oils again by splitting their long carbon chains. This process is called catalytic cracking.

▲ The Grangemouth oil refinery in Scotland, UK, is situated near to the Forth estuary where it can easily import crude oil and export refined oil products via tankers and pipelines in the North Sea.

CHOOSING AN OIL REFINERY LOCATION

Oil refineries process millions of gallons of oil that have been drilled from the Earth's crust. Choosing the location of an oil refinery is not an easy task because a number of environmental and safety concerns need to be taken into account.

The world's first oil refinery was opened in 1856 in Romania (with investment from the USA). Many more refineries followed, but during the Second World War they were heavily bombed during strategic campaigns. Today, the largest oil refinery in the world is in Saudi Arabia. It was built in Abqaiq, a city originally designed as a seaport, before the refinery took over.

Oil refineries are often located on the coast and away from busy cities. When choosing the location for an oil refinery, the following factors need to be taken into consideration:

▶ **Air pollution** – Although industries are regulated by strict controls regarding the amount of pollution they release into the atmosphere, oil refineries emit a number of polluting gases. To reduce the effects of air pollution on people, refineries should be built away from built-up areas. Care should also be taken to position the refinery so that prevailing winds do not carry pollution in the direction of towns and cities.

▶ **Water pollution** – Some refineries use water from local rivers and streams for cooling purposes. This means that the water is pumped out of the river or stream, circulated around a cooling tower and returned to the river at a higher temperature. This increase in water temperature is called thermal pollution. Some species of fish are unable to survive in these conditions. Waste products from a refinery may also be washed into local rivers and streams.

▶ **Noise pollution** – Machinery that operates 24 hours a day can make a lot of noise for people living nearby. Lorries and trains that come to pick up refined products also contribute to the noise.

▶ **Transportation** – The oil refinery must be near to rail, road or sea links and close to the site where the oil has been drilled.

▶ **Special sites of interest** – Like other buildings, oil refineries must avoid areas of special scientific interest. These can include regions where rare animals are being protected.

▶ **Available workforce** – It may be tempting to build an oil refinery in a remote location where no people or animals can be affected. However, a refinery needs workers living relatively nearby.

▶ **Available customers** – Oil refineries need to be within easy reach of customers. It is essential to have good transport links. Some refineries use pipelines as a method of transportation.

THE EFFECTS OF HURRICANE KATRINA

Sometimes, the production and refining of oil can be halted by unprecedented circumstances. In 2005, the destructive force of Hurricane Katrina in the Mississippi Delta, USA, caused some offshore oil rigs to sink and others to go adrift (below) or missing. Pipelines were ruptured, oil-storage facilities were battered and many oil refineries had to be shut down. Events like these cost the US government many billions of dollars and disrupt the oil economy around the world. When choosing the location of a new oil refinery, even the potential for natural disasters should be taken into consideration.

TEST YOURSELF

▶ Study the diagram of this fictitious island. Imagine you work for an oil company and it is your job to find a location for a new refinery for oil that is drilled out at sea. Where on the island would you build the refinery? Give reasons for your choice.

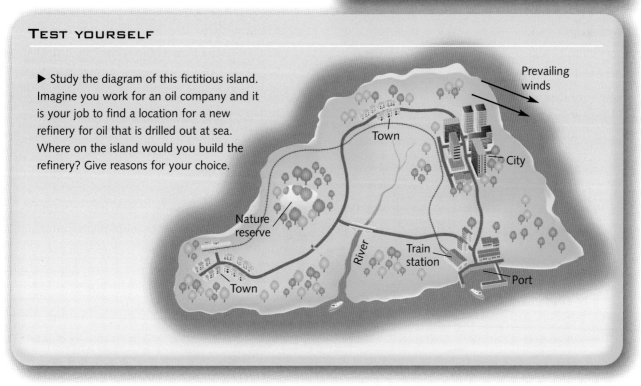

Making plastics

Fossil fuels are best known for their ability to 'power' our world by generating heat. However, in recent years, fossil fuels have been used to produce a number of common everyday materials. Plastics, for example, are a relatively new phenomenon. They form many of the objects around us – from cooking utensils and furniture to dustbins and traffic cones. Plastics are made from crude oil through a process called **polymerisation**.

DISCOVERING PLASTICS

Many natural 'plastics' such as cellulose and rubber have been used for centuries, but these products form just a small fraction of the plastics that we have available today. Over time, scientists have looked at the properties of these natural materials and have tried to improve upon them. In 1839, legend has it that an American inventor called Charles Goodyear was experimenting with sulphur and rubber and accidentally dropped a piece of sulphur into the rubber mixture.

▲ Telephones used to be made from bakelite plastic.

▲ Charles Goodyear

His mistake caused the rubber to become much stronger and able to withstand high temperatures. This later became known as vulcanised rubber and made the perfect material for car tyres (hence the name of the Goodyear tyre company).

MAKING PLASTICS

The plastics boom did not begin until the early 1900s, however, with the discovery of a brand new plastic called bakelite. In 1907, a Belgian-American chemist named Leo Baekeland mixed two chemicals together (phenol and formaldehyde). He discovered that they created a sticky mass when heated, but then cooled to give a hard substance. Baekeland had invented the first plastic that held its shape after being heated. Bakelite was a useful insulation material and its uses included covering electrical wires and making billiard balls!

Today, some plastics are made by chemically altering the composition of oil. Oils that have had hydrogen atoms removed from their carbon chains have weaker links between their atoms and can easily be converted into other products, such as plastics.

◄ Leo Baekeland

When plastics are made, the molecules in hydrocarbons are linked together to form a long chain that we call a polymer. Some hydrocarbons, called alkenes, contain double bonds between their atoms. Ethene is an example of an alkene and has the formula C_2H_4. The two carbon atoms are connected with a double bond.

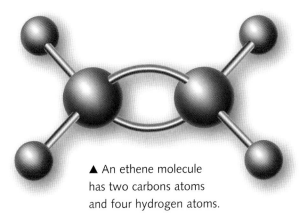

▲ An ethene molecule has two carbons atoms and four hydrogen atoms.

When ethene molecules are pressed together and a catalyst is added, one of the bonds breaks and links to another ethene molecule. In this way, many hundreds or thousands of molecules can be made to link together in a long chain, called polyethene. Polymers like this are very strong and can be made into a range of different products, such as toys and plastic bottles.

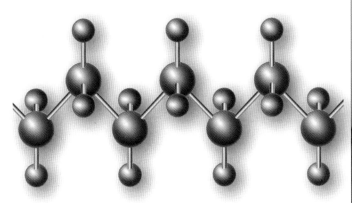

▲ During polymerisation, ethene molecules link together to form a strong plastic called polyethene.

▲ Polymers are used to make everyday plastic materials.

PLASTICS AND THE ENVIRONMENT

One of the advantages of plastic as a material is that it is very hard-wearing. Plastics break down very slowly and they are generally resistant to physical or chemical attack. However, this can have adverse consequences on the environment, making their disposal difficult. We tend to dispose of plastics in two ways:

(1) BURIED IN A LANDFILL

Because plastics are **non-biodegradable**, they will remain in the ground for many hundreds of years. This can create an ugly landscape, render the land useless for any other purpose and interrupt the natural carbon cycle.

(2) BURNT

This method is more instant in the disposal of unwanted plastics, but releases **toxic** gases into the atmosphere.

▲ Plastics remain in a landfill site for hundreds of years.

The production of plastics is also not without problems. Many plastics are made from fossil fuels. Fossil fuels are also needed to heat some of the reactions that produce plastics. These fuels can release polluting chemicals into the atmosphere.

SOLUTIONS TO THE ENVIRONMENTAL PROBLEMS

In the 1990s, plastic **recycling** programmes became more and more common, especially in the USA. Plastics can now be separated from regular rubbish, melted down and remoulded into new plastics. Unfortunately, not all plastics are suitable for this treatment – those that are have a clear 'recycling' marking on their side.

The largest drawback of plastic recycling is that the process is very labour intensive. The plastics must be sorted into individual varieties before they can be treated. This is usually done by hand. Another drawback is that, sometimes, recycling plastics is not cost-effective in financial terms. For this reason, polystyrene is very rarely recycled.

To counteract these problems, scientists have recently designed some biodegradable plastics. These plastics will break down much more readily when exposed to sunlight. The main disadvantage, however, is that the carbon within the plastic is released as carbon dioxide gas into the atmosphere which can contribute to **global warming** (see page 29). At present, biodegradable plastics are too expensive for everyday use.

TEST YOURSELF

▶ One of the advantages of using plastics has been their low cost compared to other materials such as glass and metal. However, the cost of plastic has risen dramatically in recent years. Why do you think this is?

The cost of fuels

Fossil fuels are described as non-renewable fuels. This means that they are being used up much more quickly than they can be produced. Every day, we use about 320 billion kilowatt-hours of energy – the equivalent to approximately 22 light bulbs constantly glowing for every person on the planet. Such a high-energy demand cannot be sustained indefinitely by the fossil fuels that we have left.

WHERE ARE FOSSIL FUELS FOUND?

The largest oil reserves in the world are in Venezuela, South America (which also has the second largest natural gas reserves in the western hemisphere). Venezuela exports some of this oil to the USA and meets about 15 per cent of US energy requirements. Venezuela's oil exports earn the government about half of its annual revenues. In 2006, for example, a barrel of Venezuelan crude oil was worth more than US$50.

Venezuelan natural gas, although plentiful, is not distributed as successfully, however, due to inadequate transportation. About 70 per cent of the supply is consumed by industries in Venezuela. In 2003, however, Venezuela signed a contract with neighbouring Colombia, allowing the construction of a 200-kilometre pipeline for gas distribution.

Nigeria also has a healthy supply of oil and is Africa's biggest oil exporter. Much of Nigeria's oil is found in a region called the Delta and for 50 years, oil has been extracted here, potentially earning billions of dollars. However, communities in the Delta continue to live in poverty. This has led to cases of oil theft where organised groups have siphoned oil from the pipelines and sold it on the black market.

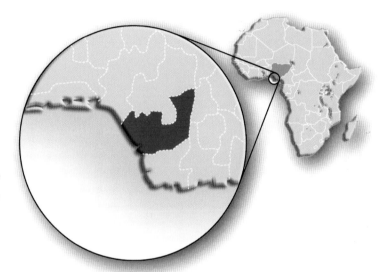

▲ Nigeria is rich in oil supplies, mainly in the Delta region.

These two cases highlight the importance of local politics in deciding the cost of oil. Countries that market their products well can potentially be sitting on a vast fortune, but oil reserves do not necessarily bring wealth.

The price of fuels is constantly changing as events around the world influence its value. In recent years, as technology has improved and countries such as China and India have begun to develop rapidly, we are using more energy resources than ever before. Oil in particular is in great demand – and because supplies are running low, prices have risen dramatically. Natural disasters and wars can also affect the price of oil by disrupting supplies.

ENVIRONMENTAL CONCERNS

Although fossil fuels have value in financial and political terms, they also have an environmental cost. When fossil fuels are burnt, the hydrocarbons that they contain combust to produce steam, carbon dioxide and carbon monoxide. Carbon dioxide is a **greenhouse gas** that contributes towards global warming (see page 29). Carbon monoxide is a poisonous gas that can be fatal (see page 9). In addition, fossil fuels release small amounts of other gases, such as nitrogen oxides and sulphur dioxide. Nitrogen oxides can produce smog and sulphur dioxide contributes to **acid rain** (see page 32).

▼ In Los Angeles, USA, the sunny climate causes car exhaust emissions and particles in the air to form smog.

▲ Oil spills can take months, even years, to clean up.

The drilling and distribution of oil can also lead to widespread destruction. The Caribbean coast of Venezuela, for example, is littered with oil debris. In other parts of the country, **subsidence** caused by excavation programmes, is also visible.

FIGHTING THE COSTS

Unfortunately, the decline of fossil fuels is inevitable. But there are many things that we can do to try to make them last longer – and to limit the effects that they have on the environment in the meantime. Some governments are trying to encourage industries to save energy by using more efficient equipment. Recycling programmes are also being developed so that recycled products are made with less energy than their 'new' counterparts. Measures are also being put into place to reduce the amount of polluting gases that industries release into the atmosphere. When financial considerations are taken into account these are not easy changes to make. Some governments are therefore trying to help by reducing taxes for 'clean' energy users.

INVESTIGATE

▶ Photochemical smog is a type of air pollution. Use the internet to find out how nitrogen oxides contribute to the smog and the health risks that smog causes. Which cities are most affected and why?

Environmental factors

You've seen the headlines. Temperatures are rising, glaciers are melting (right) and habitats are changing. But how are these stories related to the fuels that we use? Many scientists believe that recent changes in the world's climate have been caused by the rapid industrialisation of our planet. And unless we take drastic action, these trends are likely to continue for the foreseeable future.

GLOBAL WARMING

Since 1900, global temperatures have risen by 0.75°C. More worryingly, although temperatures used to be relatively constant, since 1979, temperatures on land have increased almost twice as fast as they have on sea. In 2006, we had the warmest year on record and, unless action is taken, scientists estimate that by 2050, temperatures may be rising by up to five per cent a year.

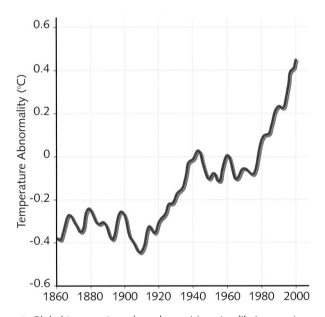

▲ Global temperatures have been rising steadily in recent years.

Scientists have been debating the reality of global warming for a number of years. Many scientists believe that human activities have drastically increased the amount of carbon dioxide in our atmosphere, as a result of the Industrial Revolution and our modern lifestyles. Other scientists think the phenomenon is just a natural change in the Earth's orbit around the Sun. They believe that the current increase in atmospheric levels of carbon dioxide is not unusual and may be caused by the end of a mini-ice age, which is naturally leading to our climate becoming warmer. Although the debate continues, many people want to take action now, to reduce the risk of potential consequences in years to come.

WHY DO TEMPERATURES RISE?

It is now widely believed that increased carbon dioxide (CO_2) emissions are causing our climate to warm up. When fossil fuels burn they release 'greenhouse gases' (such as CO_2), which rise into the atmosphere and collect forming a 'blanket' of gases. As a natural phenomenon, this blanket is very important because it helps to maintain the temperature of the Earth at a suitable level for life to exist. However, with increased use of fossil fuels, this blanket is becoming thicker, retaining heat and increasing temperatures on Earth.

When the Sun's **radiation** passes through the atmosphere it reflects from the Earth's surface. Some of the heat escapes back through the atmosphere, but some heat now remains trapped, causing temperatures to rise.

▼ An increase in greenhouse gases causes more of the Sun's radiation to become trapped in the Earth's atmosphere.

Although carbon dioxide is not the only greenhouse gas, estimates have shown that levels of carbon dioxide are now rising 200 times faster than at any time in the last 650,000 years.

THE CONSEQUENCES OF GLOBAL WARMING

The full effects of global warming are not completely known, but scientists have made the following predictions:

▶ **Effects on ecosystems** – An increase in global temperatures changes sensitive **ecosystems** and forces some species out of their habitat.

▶ **Glaciers** – Global warming has caused glaciers to melt and become smaller. For example, the ice field on the top of Mount Kilimanjaro in Tanzania, Africa, has reduced significantly in recent years. Melted glaciers can also bring a shortage of water, causing problems for countries such as China and India who rely on abundant water resources.

▲ ▼ These satellite images of Mount Kilimanjaro, Tanzania, show a significant reduction in snow and ice at the top of the mountain between 1993 (top) and 2000 (bottom). The ice cap has lost 80 per cent of its volume over the last 100 years.

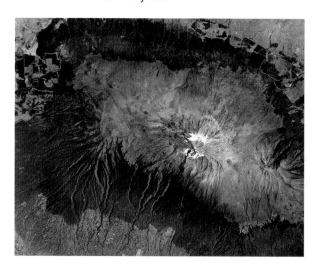

▶ **Ocean levels** – A small rise in ocean levels can make some coastal plains uninhabitable. Scientists estimate that Vietnam, Bangladesh and Indonesia could be seriously affected. Many port cities around the world are also under increased threat from flooding. London, for example, could flood if sea levels continue to rise.

▲ The Thames Barrier protects London from high tides, but will it be able to stop London from flooding in the future?

▶ **Ozone layer** – Although **CFCs** are thought to be the main cause of the destruction of the **ozone layer**, scientists think that global warming is making the ozone layer weaker. As surface temperatures rise, the higher reaches of the atmosphere will become colder, making it more difficult for the ozone layer to repair itself naturally. Scientists think that by 2030, climate change may become the main cause of reduced ozone levels.

▶ **Increase in biomass** – An increase in carbon dioxide in the atmosphere could cause plants to increase their metabolism during **photosynthesis**. This could cause an eventual increase in dead and decaying plant matter, releasing methane.

▶ **Spread of disease** – Global warming could increase the number of disease carriers such as rats (carrying plague) and mosquitoes (carrying malaria). Droughts can cause a decline in predators and changing weather patterns encourage new breeding grounds for disease carriers.

▶ **Financial effects** – It is estimated that global warming could cost insurance companies nearly US$150 billion during each year of the next decade, following an increase in flooding and forest fires, for example.

▶ **Methane gas** – As sea temperatures rise at the North and Sound Poles, another dangerous greenhouse gas – methane – could also be released. Methane is trapped in solid, ice-like compounds found in the ocean floor. This gas bubbles to the surface as temperatures rise.

ACID RAIN

Acid rain was first reported in Manchester, UK in 1852. However, despite this early identification, public awareness around the world was not increased until the 1960s, when layers of glacial ice were analysed for their gas composition. Glaciers build up in layers over time (in a similar way to sedimentary rock) and as they form, gases from the atmosphere become trapped in the ice.

Glacier analysis has shown that since the Industrial Revolution (see page 17), levels of sulphur dioxide and nitrogen oxides in the atmosphere have increased. Fossil fuels contain small amounts of impurities, such as sulphur. When fuels are burnt, these impurities combust in air to form gases (such as sulphur dioxide) that rise into the atmosphere. Sulphur dioxide is a soluble gas and will dissolve in rain clouds to form a very dilute sulphuric acid solution. We call this 'acid rain'. Other types of acid rain can be caused by carbon dioxide (which dissolves in water to produce carbonic acid) and nitrogen oxides (which dissolve in water to produce nitric acid).

▼ When fossil fuels are burnt, sulphur dioxide and nitrogen oxides are released. These gases dissolve in the atmosphere to form acid rain.

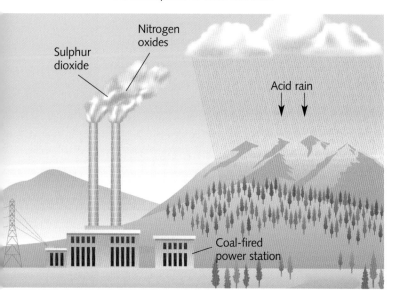

THE EFFECTS OF ACID RAIN

One of the major problems with acid rain is that it is not always a local problem – prevailing winds can easily carry it to another location. Acid rain corrodes buildings and structures and can be damaging to ecosystems:

▶ **Lakes** – Scientists have shown that there is a strong link between acidic water and declining populations of fish. Acidic water prevents key **enzymes** from working in fish larvae so they do not survive. Acid rain can also release toxic metals, such as aluminium, into lakes causing some fish to produce excess mucus that will prevent their gills from working properly. Simple plankton will also not grow in acidic water, causing a major disruption to the food chain.

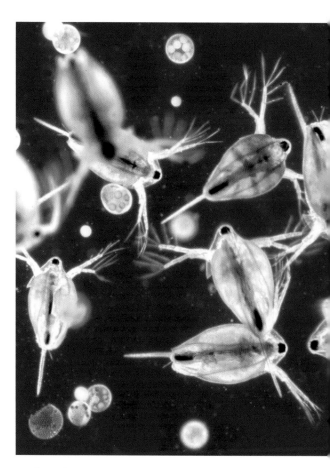

▲ These freshwater plankton form the basis of a river food chain, but acid rain is causing a decline in their numbers.

▲ Acid rain damages trees because it reacts with many nutrients in the soil that the trees need to survive.

▶ **Trees** – Acid rain can be damaging to trees. Waxy leaves break down, root growth slows and toxic metals may be consumed by the trees.

▶ **Soil** – Acid rain can leach minerals out of the soil making it unsuitable for plants to grow.

▶ **Buildings and statues** – Stonework containing calcium (such as limestone) reacts with sulphuric acid. This type of corrosion can be seen on old gravestones and churchyard statues.

▶ **Micro-organisms** – Some tropical micro-organisms readily consume acids, but others cannot survive in acidic conditions. This can affect the natural balance in ecosystems.

▶ **Metals** – Acid rain can cause rust to form on metals containing iron because the acid speeds up the **oxidation** process.

We can reduce acid rain by limiting levels of polluting gases in the atmosphere. Using low-sulphur petrol and diesel in our cars and fitting catalytic converters (to reduce levels of nitrogen dioxide emitted from the exhaust, for example) are two simple measures. On a larger scale, burning fewer fossil fuels by using alternative sources of energy (see chapter 7) is a longer-term solution.

MONITORING AIR QUALITY

Monitoring the quality of our air has become an important science. Governments now set targets for improving air quality, and pass legislation such as the Clean Air Acts in the USA and the UK, for example. Countries have their own monitoring sites to co-ordinate a nationwide picture of pollution levels. Automatic monitoring networks record pollution on a regular basis to detect any changing patterns. Scientists also look at specific pollutants affecting urban and rural areas. Two main methods are used to monitor air quality:

▶ **Passive sampling** – Passive sampling is one of the cheapest air monitoring methods and is mainly used to detect nitrogen dioxide and benzene. Sampling tubes are left open to the atmosphere, facing down to the ground to prevent any rain or dust from entering the tube. They are called 'passive' because air samples flow through the sampling tube by a process called **diffusion**. They are then collected before being analysed in a laboratory.

▶ **Active sampling** – In active sampling, a particular volume of air is pumped through a collector over a given period of time and the samples are collected daily. This type of sampling is commonly used for ozone, nitrogen oxides, sulphur dioxide and carbon monoxide. The samples are then analysed using spectroscopy to produce an accurate picture of the quantity and type of pollution that they contain.

INDICATOR SPECIES

Particular pollutants affect certain living organisms. Lichens, for example, are very sensitive to sulphur dioxide. Since the Industrial Revolution (see page 17), lichen species have reduced dramatically. Lichens absorb sulphur dioxide which then accumulates inside them causing irreversible damage.

Lichens are called **bio-indicators** because they can give us an idea of the amount of sulphur dioxide present in air. Some lichens are more tolerant to sulphur dioxide than others, so observing which lichen species are present in an area can help to estimate air quality levels. Bio-indicators can be used to monitor water pollution, too. The presence of lots of salmon or trout in a river, for example, indicates clean water.

◀ These sensors are used to measure air pollution levels. They are placed by roads or industrial plants to measure the pollution caused by vehicles or factory emissions.

Fuels of the future

Our modern lifestyles are causing us to need more and more energy. But fossil fuels will not last forever. With the ongoing decline in fossil fuels, scientists are continuing to search for new ways to provide for our energy needs in the future. We need cheap sources of energy that are also kind to the environment. With this in mind, scientists are now seriously looking at alternatives, such as nuclear energy, natural energy sources (like wind or solar energy) and hydrogen gas.

HYDROGEN – THE FUEL OF THE FUTURE?

Hydrogen is considered to be a serious alternative to fossil fuels. Hydrogen is present in many substances, but the most common source of hydrogen is water (H_2O). The oceans, for example, could provide an endless supply of hydrogen fuel. Hydrogen is also a 'clean' supply of energy. When hydrogen burns it does not pollute the atmosphere because the only combustion product is water. Hydrogen is also very light and it releases a great deal of energy. For this reason, it is ideal for use in spacecraft because a relatively small amount of fuel can power a surprisingly long journey.

▲ Hydrogen gas could be an economical way to keep this space shuttle in orbit for long periods of time.

Hydrogen can also be used to power cars. Instead of using a traditional combustion engine (which releases pollutants such as carbon dioxide), hydrogen cars use a hydrogen **fuel cell**. While batteries use up substances internally to work, fuel cells use external substances, such as hydrogen and oxygen, and continue to work indefinitely as long as a fuel source is readily available. Hydrogen is stored in the vehicle and is mixed with oxygen from the air to generate heat and electricity in a chemical reaction. Water is also produced during this process. The electricity is used to run the engine to power the wheels. Fuel cells are about 50 per cent more efficient than the average internal combustion engine. Hydrogen also burns more safely than petrol.

THE DISADVANTAGES OF HYDROGEN

▶ Although hydrogen is plentiful in the form of water, it has to be separated from water using a process called **electrolysis**. This is very expensive.

▶ Hydrogen is a 'clean' fuel but the energy needed for electrolysis comes from burning fossil fuels, which can be very polluting.

▶ At the moment, fuel cells are very expensive so hydrogen cars are not easily affordable.

▶ Unless hydrogen gas is compressed and liquefied, large tanks are needed to store and transport it.

► Energy is needed to compress hydrogen gas (and the efficiency of the resulting hydrogen product is slightly reduced). Compression also carries the risk of explosion. To overcome this latter problem, special reinforced tanks are constructed. This increases the price of hydrogen even further.

▲ These hydrogen gas tanks are used to store compressed hydrogen gas safely, but this is expensive.

CURRENT PROGRAMMES

Some countries are taking hydrogen fuel very seriously. Sweden, for example, is planning to become completely oil-free within the next 20 years and will rely solely on alternative energy sources, such as hydrogen. Iceland has committed itself to become the world's first hydrogen economy by 2050. Iceland currently imports all its hydrocarbon energy sources. However, Iceland also has a large **geothermal** resource that makes the local cost of electricity cheaper than the price of hydrocarbons. Surplus electricity in Iceland is converted into hydrocarbon replacements, such as hydrogen. Since 2002, Iceland has produced around 2,000 tonnes of hydrogen every year.

Another pilot project is being undertaken on a Norwegian island. Here, wind power is being used to generate hydrogen that is then stored. When there is little wind available, the hydrogen power is used as an alternative energy source.

In December 2005, the UK began to run some fuel cell buses in central London. These buses cause less pollution than those that use conventional fossil fuels. Other fuel cell buses are now being used in Europe and the USA. We must wait to see whether the disadvantages of hydrogen can be overcome, to produce a viable fuel for the future.

▲ This bus in Iceland is powered by a fuel cell that runs on hydrogen gas.

DID YOU KNOW?

► In 2005, 55 million tonnes of hydrogen were produced globally. This is the equivalent to about 190 million tonnes of oil. Hydrogen production is expected to rise about ten per cent every year.

► An American company has successfully completed test flights for an aircraft operating completely on liquid hydrogen. The hydrogen is stored on board and oxygen is collected during the flight. Together, these gases react in fuel cells to generate the power needed to propel the aircraft. The company claim that one tank of fuel will keep the aircraft airborne for 24 hours.

TEST YOURSELF

▶ At the moment, we burn fossil fuels to create the energy needed to produce hydrogen from water. What other sources of energy could be used instead, that are kinder to the environment?

GASOHOL AND HYBRID CARS

Some countries in the world make better use of their petrol by mixing it with 10 per cent ethanol to form a mixture called gasohol. This mixture is sometimes called E10 and can be used in car engines without any extra adaptation. Denmark, for example, uses the fuel nationwide and Brazil now produces over 16 billion litres of ethanol – using half its sugar harvest to fuel cars.

MAKING GASOHOL

Until 1975, Brazil relied heavily on imported oil to meet its energy needs that were growing rapidly. However, with the increasing price of oil, the Brazilian government made the decision to make a big investment in gasohol production.

The glucose in sugar cane can be converted into ethanol through the process of fermentation. This process is cheaper than obtaining ethanol from the fractional distillation of alcohol solutions. Brazilian farmers are now awarded generous subsidies for growing sugar cane.

The equation for this reaction is:

Glucose $\longrightarrow$ Ethanol + Carbon dioxide

$$C_6H_{12}O_{6(s)} \longrightarrow 2C_2H_5OH_{(l)} + 2CO_{2(g)}$$

Brazil has a hot, tropical climate and sugar cane grows easily there. However, ethanol production is not financially viable in all countries because it depends on favourable weather conditions.

HYBRID CARS

A hybrid vehicle is one that has its own onboard rechargeable energy storage system. Mopeds, for example, can combine the power of petrol with the pedal power of the rider to propel them. Trains are now commonly diesel-electric hybrids. In Seattle, USA, overhead electric wires are used to power diesel-electric buses. Some of the cars on our roads are petrol-electric hybrid cars.

All roadworthy cars need to be able to drive over 400 kilometres before they need refuelling, be refuelled quickly and easily, and keep up with other traffic on the road. Petrol and diesel cars meet these requirements, but they also produce a lot of pollution. A hybrid car significantly reduces the amount of greenhouse emissions, whilst maintaining these other desirable features.

HOW DO THEY WORK?

A hybrid car can work in one of two ways.
(1) It can either use stored petrol, or stored electricity in a battery, to start the motor. Once the motor is running, both the petrol and the electricity can be used to power the vehicle.
(2) Petrol is used to turn a generator but the car is powered by electricity. The generator produces electricity for storage in the car's batteries.

DID YOU KNOW?

▶ Ethanol can also be produced from the fermentation of corn. However, some people think this is a waste of food. The amount of corn needed to fill a 60 litre fuel tank with ethanol will feed one person for six months.

▶ About 50 million tonnes of US corn goes into ethanol production every year. This is nearly one-sixth of the country's grain harvest, but will supply only three per cent of its vehicle fuel.

▲ Wind farms tend to be located in remote, flat or high areas where winds are strong and urban areas are least affected.

THE POWER OF NATURE

Natural energy sources, such as wind and tidal energy, have been developed over recent years as a potential source of 'clean' energy for our future. However, at present, these energy sources do not produce large amounts of power (electricity) and it is difficult to persuade governments to use them. This may change however, with fossil fuels continuing to decline and the search for clean alternative energy sources becoming more important than ever before.

WIND POWER

In 2005, wind power contributed approximately one per cent of the world's energy needs. Wind power is generated through large turbines that convert movement into electricity through a generator. Wind energy has traditionally been used for many years – windmills, for example, have been used to crush grain or to pump water.

▲ Windmills have traditionally been used to capture energy. They use the strength of the wind to turn machinery.

ADVANTAGES AND DISADVANTAGES

Wind energy is a good alternative energy source because it does not rely on fossil fuels or produce polluting gases. This source of energy is also unlikely to run out and the electricity that it generates can be stored for later use. However, a large number of wind turbines are needed to produce a significant amount of electricity. Many people think that groups of turbines (or 'wind farms') are ugly and spoil the landscape. For this reason, many wind turbines are located out at sea, away from urban activity. The turbines may also pose a danger to migrating birds that accidentally fly into their path. Wind turbines are built in areas where the wind speed is greater than 20 kilometres per hour. These areas tend to be at high altitudes, on flat surfaces or out at sea.

Germany, Spain, India, Denmark and the USA currently have the largest investments in wind power. Denmark also has a large market in wind turbine exports.

WATER

Water is a natural resource that can be transformed into electrical power. Water power currently makes about a sixth of the world's electricity. In a **hydroelectric** power station, river water is collected by a dam and then flows from a height through turbines to generate electricity. Power stations can also use ocean water to generate electricity, capturing the power of the waves or the tides that move across the ocean.

ADVANTAGES AND DISADVANTAGES

Water is another renewable source of energy that can generate significant amounts of power. If the proposed tidal barrage on the Severn estuary in Bristol, UK, is built for example, it is estimated that 18 million tonnes of coal can be saved for every year it is in operation.

However, hydroelectric power can also bring problems. Dams can stop fish and other animals from moving up and down rivers. Changes in the flow of water can also cause salt levels and the

TEST YOURSELF

▶ Draw up a table listing the advantages and disadvantages of each of the alternative energy sources described on pages 35 to 45.

amount of sunlight that penetrates the water to change. These factors can have a knock-on effect on the food chain. Dams can also cause flooding. When some plants become submerged by floodwater they decompose quickly, releasing methane gas. This is another greenhouse gas thought to contribute towards global warming.

▼ Large ocean turbines use the energy of moving water to generate electricity.

GEOTHERMAL ENERGY

Geothermal energy (the heat from the Earth's crust) can be used to generate electricity. In some parts of the world, there are hot rocks beneath the Earth's surface. Water pipes are passed through the hot rocks (or cold water is pumped into the ground to absorb the heat), which creates hot water for homes.

In other countries, such as Iceland, thermal pools are utilised. Wells are drilled and the upward flow of hot water or steam can be used to generate electricity. It is estimated that Iceland can produce significant amounts of geothermal energy for another 100 years.

Changing levels of heat in the world's oceans can also be used to generate power. The oceans absorb energy from the Sun and this makes surface waters warmer than deeper areas. A new technology called Ocean Thermal Energy Conversion (OTEC) uses these differences in temperatures to generate electricity.

ADVANTAGES AND DISADVANTAGES

Geothermal power can be produced very cost effectively in areas such as Africa. In Kenya, for example, two large geothermal plants have been built with plans for a third. Together, these are estimated to provide 25 per cent of Kenya's energy demands and they reduce the country's reliance on imported oil.

However, using geothermal energy can cause minor movements in the Earth's crust and could increase the risk of earthquakes. This is particularly the case if cold water is injected into the ground. The cooling effect of the water also makes the geothermal energy a less 'renewable' resource.

SOLAR POWER

The amount of energy reaching the Earth from the Sun each day is around 10,000 times the world's current daily energy demand. We can now capture some of this energy to make electricity. Solar cells absorb the Sun's radiation and release **electrons** to create an electric current. Solar energy can also be used to heat water circulating in pipes that are painted matt black to absorb as much radiation as possible. At the moment, the amount of solar energy we can capture is limited, however. This may change in the coming years as technology develops. Some houses are built with solar panels on the roof to provide extra electrical energy at home. In the future, perhaps our cars will run on solar power?

▲ Solar panels can produce extra electricity for a home.

TIME TRAVEL: INTO THE FUTURE

▶ Solar energy is currently used in space to power spacecraft and satellites. The energy is captured using solar panels similar to those described on this page. Scientists think that in the future, solar satellites might be able to gather solar energy and send it back to Earth using microwave beams. If the solar energy was then converted into electricity, it could become an endless supply of clean power.

NUCLEAR POWER

Nuclear energy was first discovered by accident in 1896 by the French scientist Henri Becquerel. Becquerel found some photographic plates that had been stored near uranium and noticed they had become changed in ways similar to that of light exposure. This discovery paved the way for many years of research, leading to today's use of nuclear energy as a source of electricity generation.

▲ Henri Becquerel

▲ Nuclear power stations currently generate about 17 per cent of the world's electricity.

WHAT IS NUCLEAR POWER?

The neutrons and protons in the nucleus of an atom are held together by very strong forces. When a heavy nucleus is spilt, these forces are overcome and a lot of energy is released. This is called **nuclear fission** and is the type of nuclear energy produced in most power stations. Energy can also be produced when two lighter nuclei are joined together. We call this **nuclear fusion**.

Nuclear energy is produced by a fuel called uranium. Uranium is found in rocks in the ground but has to be refined before it can be used as a nuclear fuel. Nuclear energy is generated in a nuclear reactor, a large tank or building inside a nuclear power station. Here, uranium atoms are split (or fused) to release energy. When the atoms split, particles are released which strike other uranium atoms, causing them to split also. However, the reactions are carried out in controlled conditions at a steady rate.

The energy released is then used to heat water to make steam to spin a turbine and power a generator to produce electricity. Some countries, such as France, depend on nuclear energy for most of their electricity. However, other governments find it difficult to balance the advantages and disadvantages of nuclear power. With an urgent need to find alternatives to fossil fuels, however, nuclear power may become popular.

ADVANTAGES

▶ Although nuclear reactors are very expensive to build, only a small amount of fuel is needed to produce energy – one kilogramme of uranium, for example, produces as much energy as 3,000 tonnes of coal! Once a reactor has been built, nuclear power can therefore be considered to be a cheap source of electricity.

▶ Nuclear energy is thought to be a 'clean' source of energy because it does not produce polluting gases from burning fuels.

▶ Nuclear power stations can help a country to have control over its own energy (rather than relying on imports from abroad).

▶ This type of 'alternative' electricity generation does not rely on weather patterns (which are vital to wind or solar power, for example).

DISADVANTAGES

▶ Many people worry about the safety of nuclear energy, particularly after high profile disasters such as at Chernobyl, Ukraine, in 1986. Safety standards have greatly improved over the last 30 years but some people think this is not enough.

▼ In 1986, human error caused the meltdown of the Chernobyl nuclear reactor in Ukraine – the world's worst nuclear disaster.

▶ Mining for uranium can scar the natural landscape. Large quantities of rock have to be mined in order to find small deposits of uranium. This can destroy natural habitats.

▶ Fossil fuels are still used during part of the nuclear process – from mining, to transportation and waste disposal.

▶ Nuclear waste remains radioactive (and dangerous) for thousands of years. Managing this waste (see below) is problematic and very expensive. In the UK, for example, it is estimated that it will cost around £70 billion to clean up the country's decommissioned nuclear power stations.

▶ Power stations are targets for terrorist attacks. The materials used in nuclear fuel are highly radioactive and can make people very ill. Security at nuclear power stations has to be very tight. The technology could also easily be adapted to produce nuclear weapons that cause untold devastation.

NUCLEAR WASTE

Nuclear reactors produce some materials that cannot be used again. Unfortunately, these materials remain radioactive for thousands of years. Nuclear fuels are first cooled in special ponds in the nuclear power station but it can take up to 50 years for them to cool down! Once they are cooled, the fuels are dissolved in acid so they can be disposed of more safely. The waste is then turned into powder and stored in strong metal containers.

A more permanent solution to the problem is to bury the waste deep underground. At present, the Canadian government is considering a plan

▲ These fuel rods are being cooled in a special pond at a nuclear power station.

to dig a vault between 500 and 1,000 metres underground, in stable geological formations. Nuclear waste would then be stored in the vaults in corrosion-resistant containers. In the USA, there are also plans to bury nuclear waste in the Nevada Desert. However, people living close by are worried about having radioactive materials in the area.

▶ Some nuclear waste is turned into a dry powder and stored in strong metal containers. Nuclear waste stores are not popular with local residents, however.

Time travel: Biofuels

One of the more exciting areas of research into renewable fuels is our use of biomass – energy from the Sun that becomes incorporated into animals and plants via the food chain. Biomass fuels (or 'biofuels') can be burnt to release energy. Although the technology is still being developed, as a widespread source of renewable and clean energy, biofuels have the potential to become significant fuels of the future.

Sources of biofuels

Plant resources, such as wood, straw and charcoal, are an abundant source of biofuels. Some crops are specifically grown for the production of biofuels. These include corn, soya beans and rapeseed.

▲ These soya bean pods contain energy we can use.

▲ These wood chips are used for biofuel production.

Although these fuels release carbon dioxide when they are burnt, they also absorb carbon dioxide as they grow. This balances the amount of carbon dioxide in the atmosphere.

Vegetable and animal fats are also a source of biofuel. Vegetable oils come from seeds, nuts and fruits (such as sunflower seeds, peanuts and olives) and many animals store fat under their skin. Lastly, biofuels can be made from waste material, such as animal faeces, forestry waste or rotting rubbish, providing a useful answer to some of the world's waste management problems.

Ocean plants can also be used as biofuels. Seaweed, such as *Sargassum* and *Sostera* grow up to 60 centimeres a day. Scientists think that huge seaweed farms could be used to absorb vast quantities of carbon dioxide during photosynthesis, and then harvested as a source of biofuel.

▼ Rapeseed is another common source of biofuel.

▼ Sargassum seaweed grows very quickly.

USES FOR BIOFUELS

Together, biofuel sources currently generate approximately 15 per cent of the world's energy. At the moment, biofuels are most commonly used in domestic cooking and heating. Some homeowners in the USA, for example, burn corn in special stoves to reduce their energy bills. Biofuels, such as biogas, can also be used to generate electricity. Biogas is made from animal and human waste and rotting plant matter. It can even be collected from rotting waste material in compost heaps or landfill sites. Biogas is mostly methane. It can be used for heating and lighting, but is mostly used to generate electricity.

THE ADVANTAGES OF BIOFUELS

▶ Using biofuels helps to save on natural energy resources such as coal, oil and gas.

▶ Biofuels can be made from a variety of natural resources. Biodiesel, for example, can be made from palm, cottonseed, sunflower and peanut oil. Biodiesel can also be made from recycled cooking grease!

▶ Biofuels emit low levels of greenhouse gases when they are burnt.

▶ When biofuels are used as a car fuel they are very efficient, improving mileage by up to three per cent. They also produce less exhaust emissions. Biodiesel can be used in any diesel engine with very little modification.

▶ The energy that biofuels contain can be stored for long periods of time without loss of energy.

▶ More crops can be grown to replace harvested crops, which means such biofuels are renewable. This can help the agricultural community. Crops also absorb carbon dioxide (CO_2) when they grow (balancing the amount of CO_2 released when they are burnt).

▶ Biofuels could help to reduce our dependency on foreign oil imports.

▶ Biofuels are biodegradable – if they are spilt or disposed of in the ground, they decompose fairly easily.

▲ Biofuels are a lot kinder to the environment than traditional fossil fuels.

THE DISADVANTAGES OF BIOFUELS

▶ Biofuels can be unreliable when used at both high and low temperatures. They can break down when they are hot and may solidify when cold. This would be a problem when used in vehicles, for example.

▶ Biodiesel is a type of biofuel made from crops such as corn, sunflowers or soya beans. As it passes through a car engine, it can release deposits that then clog up filters. Biodiesel can also corrode rubber components.

▶ Biofuels release methane gas. This is a greenhouse gas that contributes to global warming.

▶ At the moment, biofuels are expensive to produce. Soya bean oil and rapeseed oil are currently the only cheap source.

MODIFYING BIOFUELS

Despite their advantages, biofuels are not used as a major source of energy in many countries because the convenience of current fuels, such as oil and gas, are a more appealing short-term option. Scientists are trying to modify biofuels to make them more useful to us in the future. Researchers at the US department of Agriculture, for example, have successfully modified soya bean oil to make it more effective at varying temperatures. In the coming years, other modifications to biofuels may make these some of the most exciting fuels for future generations.

Glossary

ACID RAIN – Rain that contains high levels of nitric or sulphuric acid. Acid rain forms when gases from industrial fuels combine with moisture in the atmosphere.

BIODEGRADABLE – The decomposition of material through the action of organisms.

BIO-INDICATORS – Biological species that cannot tolerate certain levels of pollution.

BIOMASS – Dead organisms used for fuel.

CFCs – Chlorofluorocarbons. CFCs are chemical compounds widely used in industry. When CFCs enter the atmosphere, they release chlorine which causes damage to the Earth's ozone layer.

COMBUSTION REACTION – A burning reaction.

COMPOUND – A substance consisting of two (or more) elements chemically joined together.

CONDENSE – To change from a gas to a liquid. Condensation occurs when gases are cooled.

CRUDE OIL – Untreated oil.

DIFFUSION – The movement of particles from areas of high concentration to areas of low concentration.

ECOSYSTEM – A collection of living things and the environment in which they live.

ELECTROLYSIS – Using electricity to split up chemical compounds.

ELECTRON – The negatively-charged part of an atom.

ENZYMES – Proteins in living organisms that help to speed up chemical reactions.

FERMENTATION – A reaction in which sugar is converted into alcohol.

FOOD CHAIN – The way in which a series of organisms depend on each other for sources of food.

FOSSIL FUELS – Fuels that derive from the fossilised remains of prehistoric plants and animals. Coal, oil and gas are fossil fuels.

ANSWERS

p17 Investigate
You should find that paraffin produces more energy than ethanol.

p19 Test yourself
(1) The lighter fractions came off sooner than the darker fractions and so contain fewer carbon atoms.

(2) Use the table on p19 to check your answer.

p23 Test yourself
The refinery is best placed on the east side of the port. This location is close to transport routes and would have an abundance of workers from the city nearby. Oil that is drilled out at sea could be transported to the refinery very easily. If the refinery was placed here, the prevailing winds would also blow the refinery fumes out to sea.

p26 Test yourself
The cost of plastic is a result of the cost of oil that it is derived from. Oil prices have risen due to reasons such as war, dwindling supplies and increased demand.

p28 Investigate
Sunlight and emissions such as nitrogen oxide react giving a fine film that we know as smog. This hangs low over areas where the chemicals are produced.

The smog can cause respiratory problems in some people.

Cities such as London and Los Angeles (where there are lots of traffic fumes) are most affected. Cities such as Los Angeles also have a sunny climate, contributing to the effect.

p32 Test yourself
Prevailing winds carry clouds containing acid rain from countries west of Scandinavia, such as the UK.

p37 Test yourself
Other sources of energy could be developed, such as nuclear energy, solar energy, wind energy and water energy.

p39 Test yourself
Answers can be found in the text but may include some of the following factors:

Advantages: plentiful; clean; light; renewable; cost-effective; reduced reliance on fossil fuels; made from waste material; reduced risk of greenhouse gases, global warming and damage to the ozone layer.

FUEL CELL – A device, like a battery, that generates electricity via a chemical reaction. Fuel cells use external substances, such as hydrogen and oxygen.

GEOTHERMAL – The internal heat of the Earth.

GLOBAL WARMING – The warming of the Earth's climate, thought to be caused by gases in the atmosphere trapping heat from the Sun.

GREENHOUSE GAS – A gas that contributes to global warming, such as carbon dioxide and methane.

HYDROCARBONS – Compounds that contain only hydrogen and carbon atoms.

HYDROELECTRICITY – Electricity generated by the energy of running water. Hydroelectric power stations use dams to capture and store large quantities of water.

METHANE – A gas made from carbon and hydrogen that can be used as a fuel.

NON-BIODEGRADABLE – A substance that takes many hundreds of years to break down.

Disadvantages: expensive; may still rely on burning polluting fossil fuels for extraction; not easily stored or transported; unreliable; can be dangerous; limited availability; unable to produce significant amounts of energy; damages the natural landscape; risk of damage to local wildlife or the balance of ecosystems; may depend on weather patterns (e.g. wind, solar).

NON-RENEWABLE – A substance that is not easily replaced.

NUCLEAR FISSION – The process of splitting an atom's nucleus in two, to release energy.

NUCLEAR FUSION – The process of joining two atoms' nuclei together, to release energy.

OXIDATION – A reaction in which oxygen is gained.

OZONE LAYER – A part of the atmosphere (about 15-30 km in altitude) containing ozone. Ozone is a gas which absorbs ultraviolet radiation from the Sun.

PHOTOSYNTHESIS – The process in green plants in which carbon dioxide is converted into oxygen.

POLYMERISATION – A process of making plastics.

RADIATION – The transmission of energy through space. Energy from the Sun travels to the Earth as radiation, for example.

RECYCLING – The process of re-using materials.

REFINE – The process of purifying a substance.

SPECTROSCOPY – The study of light energy and radiation in matter.

SUBSIDENCE – When part of the Earth sinks down due to movements or underground excavations.

TOXIC – Capable of causing injury or death by poison.

Useful websites:
www.bbc.co.uk/schools
www.chem4kids.com
www.sciencenewsforkids.org
www.newscientist.com
www.howstuffworks.com

Index